Mastering Coffee:

Awaken the Barista Within You and Make Exotic Coffee Drinks at Home

Marissa Marie

Contents

Basics of Coffee Making

Coffee has been one of humanity's most favoured drinks for centuries now. It was the Boston Tea Party in 1773 that really kicked off America's love for coffee, and coffee has remained the national drink ever since.

Today, It is hard to take a stroll through a city in America, or anywhere else in the world without coming across a coffee shop. Most of these coffee shops sell more than just standard coffee drinks. Most people who enter these shops, are also almost never interested in the standard coffee cup. Most of the customers of these shops seek exotic versions of the standard coffee drinks. These exotic versions have exotic names such as- Cappuccino Royale, Espresso con Panna, Mochaccino, Latte Macchiato, etc. The list is endless. You will find lots of coffee shops with coffee drinks you've never even heard of, and recipes and blends of coffee you've never even tasted.

Just like any other ingredient, you can a lot with coffee. It is up to your imagination really, but in order to awaken your imagination, you will do well to learn what others have come up with before you, and that is what this book is for. There are plenty of well-known insanely delicious exotic and gourmet coffee drinks that already exist, and in this book, I will teach you everything you need to know to start making these recipes right at home!

Once you get a hang of gourmet coffee recipes, you are ready to start experimenting, and making your own gourmet coffee recipes tailored exactly to your own needs!

Know the Coffee Beans

All coffee beans are not made equal. Different geographical locations yield different varieties of coffee beans, and different varieties vary in flavour. For example, the Coffea arabica plant, which grows at high altitudes throughout the equatorial regions of the world, is considered the best coffee you can get your hands on today. Today, Central America, South America, and Africa are its greatest producers.

Another species of coffee plant, Coffea robusta, is also grown primarily in Africa, but this plant is used mostly for the lower grades of coffee that are on the market today.

These two are the most economically important varieties of coffee plant are the Arabica and the Robusta. Approximately 60% of the coffee produced worldwide is Arabica and 40% is Robusta. Arabica beans consist of 0.8–1.4% caffeine and Robusta beans consist of 1.7–4% caffeine.

Within the same species, there is plenty of variation depending on the geographical location of the place where it is grown. The flavours vary because of the variance in altitude, rainfall, and soil quality.

The coffee beans we get to see are usually brown in colour, but they weren't always that way. Coffee beans are green at the time of harvest. These green beans are then roasted at around 400°F for approximately 5 to 15 minutes depending on the temperature, while rotating them in large bins.

Most beans are light or medium roasted, resulting in a light- or medium-brown colour and mild taste. Viennese or dark-roasted coffee results in a darker brown bean and a virtually burnt, yet tangy taste. The darkest roast- called espresso, Italian, or French- has a dark brown to virtually black colour and a burnt to charcoaly taste.

The amount of roasting brings in another layer of variation to the coffee. So, there can be multiple coffee types within the same species. Now, most of the coffee drinks and beans you buy from the market aren't just one coffee species roasted uniformly. Instead, most of the coffee you buy is a blend of different species roasted to different degrees.

For example, the most common coffee we find today is called "Mocha Java", which as the name suggests is a blend of Arabica coffee from Mocha (in Yemen) and Java (Indonesia).

As the popularity of coffee has grown, so have new trends. One of the most popular new trends we see today in the world of coffee is that of flavoured coffee beans. Today, there are multiple flavoured coffee beans available in the market such as- Vanilla Nut, Chocolate Almond, and Irish Cream. These come in handy, but you can achieve the same result by adding the flavour to the drink during preparation. This way you have more flexibility. When preparing flavoured coffee, make sure you put in flavours that go with each other.

Another trend we see on the rise today is that of decaffeinated coffee. Back in the day, one needed to settle with low quality coffee beans for a decaf. Today, however, no such compromise needs to be made as you can find delicious high quality decaf varieties of coffee beans quite easily. This has primarily happened due to the refinement of the decaffeination process. One of the most prevalent decaffeination processes today uses a chemical solvent (most commonly methylene chloride) that dissolves with the caffeine and can then be discarded, together with the caffeine. Another popular process is the swiss water process, which uses water as a solvent. However, this process is much slower and is required to be done multiple times for complete decaffeination

Storing Your Coffee Beans

Coffee doesn't last forever, and as any other perishable item, should be stored properly. Expired beans do not make the best cup of coffee.

Once the coffee beans are grinded into their powdered form, their surface area increases exponentially, and so does the rate at which they spoil. Hence, the best course of action is to store the coffee beans in their whole form, and grind instantly before you make a drink.

If you like to buy ground coffee from the market, make sure the containers are airtight. Once you open these airtight containers, it is best to consume the contents of the container within two weeks. Hence, it is best to buy pre-ground coffee in small batches.

If you buy whole coffee beans from the market, they should be stored in the freezer in an airtight container. They will keep for more than a month that way. Take two weeks' worth of beans out of the freezer and grind them. These ground beans should also be stored in airtight containers, preferably in a fridge. For maximum freshness, make sure the ground beans don't last longer than two weeks.

Basic Types of Coffee

There are two basic types of coffee that I have used in this book: brewed coffee and espresso.

Brewed coffee usually involves running hot water through coffee grounds, though it can be made using a cold-water process too. Most of the time brewed coffee is prepared using light- or medium-roast coffee, or with a dark roast like Viennese or French.

Espresso coffee mostly uses the darkest roast of coffee bean and the technique involves running hot water rapidly through finely ground espresso beans. This produces a small cup of very strong-tasting coffee that generally needs to be sweetened with at least a slight amount of sugar.

Tips for Making Insanely Delicious Coffee Drinks

Here's what you can do to get the most out of your coffee beans:-

1. Make sure the water you use is fresh and pure.
2. Normally, you should use 2 tablespoons of ground coffee for every 6 ounces of brewed coffee that you want to make. To make espresso, you generally use approximately 1 tablespoon of coffee for 1.5 ounces of espresso.
3. Always use the appropriate grind for the equipment that you're using. Too fine a grind will lead to over-extraction, blockage of your filter, or small particles of coffee beans seeping into your cup of coffee. Too coarse a grind will cause under-extraction and a weak, bitter cup of coffee as the water will go through the coffee too quickly.
4. If you are using a manual device, use water that is just off the boil, so that it does not "burn" the coffee.
5. Always serve your coffee instantly after you make it; never reheat your coffee or reuse your coffee grounds. If you want to use your hot coffee later, pour it into a preheated thermos instantly after it's brewed.
6. Make sure you clean your equipment frequently, so that coffee residues or mineral deposits don't build up. That can ruin your future cups of coffee.

7. Make sure you never leave your coffee on the burner for more than 20 minutes. That will ruin it.

Know Your Filters

If you're in the market for a new coffee filter, you should know all the options available, and their advantages and disadvantages. The most common types of filters you'll find are those made with chlorine- or oxygen-bleached white paper, unbleached brown paper, or no paper at all (also-called gold filter).

Today, the oxygen-bleached white filters rapidly gaining popularity because they are "friendly" to the environment. Brown filters, although environmentally friendly, tend to leave a faint papery taste in the coffee. Gold filters are actually made of gold-plated steel and are popular because they don't need to be replaced and don't filter out the natural oils of the coffee bean, as the paper filters do.

Know the Grind

Coffee can be ground in multiple ways, and it is extremely important do to it the right way, depending on the brewing method you intend to use.

The coarsest grind is used for percolators, French presses, and for the cold-water method of making coffee. Medium grinds are used for flat-bottomed drip makers and stove-top espresso makers. Fine grinds are used for cone-shaped drip filters, and very fine grinds are generally used for espresso machines. An extremely fine or powdery grind is used for making Turkish coffee in a jezve.

Know Your Measurements

American cooks use standard containers, the 8-ounce cup and a tablespoon that takes exactly 16 level fillings to fill that cup level. Measuring by cup makes it very difficult to give weight equivalents, as the density plays an important role when it comes to weight. The easiest way therefore to deal with cup measurements in recipes is to take the amount by volume rather than by weight. Thus, the equation reads:

1 cup = 240ml = 8 fluid Ounces

½ cup = 120ml = 4 fluid ounces

It is possible to buy a set of American cup measures in major stores around the world.

In the States, butter is sometimes measured in sticks. One stick is the equivalent of 8 tablespoons. One tablespoon of butter is therefore the equivalent to ½ ounce/15 grams.

Liquid Measures

1 Teaspoon= 5 Millilitres

1 Tablespoon = 14 millilitres

2 Tablespoons= 1 Fluid Ounce

Solid Measures

1 Ounce= 28 Grams

16 Ounces= 1 Pound

Methods for Brewing Coffee

All those who have been making gourmet coffee recipes for a while have their favourite method of brewing coffee. If you're new, you might want to try all methods out and pick one that best fits your personal preference. There are many ways of making coffee out there, but we will only discuss the best ones.

The most popular way of making coffee today is the drip method—either using a manual device by heating the water separately, or by using an electric machine. In this method, hot water is poured over the coffee grounds, which are kept in a filter over the carafe. This method is easy to follow and delivers a high-quality cup of coffee.

In te French press (or plunger pot) method, you start by placing the coffee grounds at the bottom of a glass cylinder, pouring hot water over the grounds, allowing them to steep for 2 to 4 minutes, and then dipping a steel-mesh filter down to the bottom of the cylinder. This traps the grounds on the bottom and leaves the brewed coffee on top. Then you simply pour the coffee out of the carafe. This method is popular as it requires no paper filters and all of the coffee beans' essential oils stay in your cup of coffee, resulting in a rich flavour.

For the vacuum method of making coffee you will need two glass pots that are placed over the other and are connected using a glass tube with a filter. Water is poured into the bottom pot and coffee grounds in the top, and when the water is heated, it rises through the tube and spills over the grounds. The heat is then turned off and the brewed coffee falls back through the tube into the lower pot. This technique makes an Ultra rich cup of coffee, just like the French press method. However, due to the complexity, it is not used too commonly.

For the Neapolitan flip-drip method, you will need two metal cylinders that are connected to each other, one on top of the other, with a filter in between. Water is poured in the bottom container and brought to a boil; then the entire device is turned upside down and the hot water drips down into the empty container through ground coffee in the filter. The coffee collected in this empty container is rich and tastes somewhat in between that produced by the gold filter and that produced by a stove-top espresso maker.

And finally, for the cold-water method, cold water is poured over very coarsely ground coffee in a large container and is allowed to steep for 10 to 24 hours, depending on how strong you want your coffee to be. Then the coffee is filtered into a carafe. You can store this coffee in the fridge for up to 3 weeks. This type of coffee can be drunk hot by using approximately 1/3 cup of concentrate in every cup of hot water, or you can use it in iced coffee as you would extra-strength, chilled coffee made with any hot-water process (see the following on making iced coffee). The result is a smooth, mild cup of coffee which is very low in acidity, as the cold-water process does not extract the oils of the coffee bean as thoroughly as does the hot-water process.

In order to make iced coffee using a standard hot-water brewing method, simply use 1.5 to 2 times the normal amount of coffee, brew it as you normally would, and pour it over ice—either instantly or after the coffee has cooled down to room temperature. It is best to use coffee made with this technique within 1 or 2 hours—no more than 3.

You can store this type of coffee in the fridge using an airtight container, but after approximately 1 day, the freshness and flavour of the coffee deteriorate drastically. Hence, it is always a good idea to brew your iced coffee as soon as you can before drinking it. You may also make coffee ice cubes using this mixture—or with cold-brewed coffee—that will not dilute your cup of iced coffee as regular ice cubes will.

Making Espresso

Today, expresso is commonly made in two ways- using a stovetop expresso makes or using an electric machine.

The stove-top espresso maker heats water in the lowermost chamber until it is forced up through the filter, which contains grounds of espresso roast coffee. Once the espresso reaches the top chamber, it can be conveniently poured out through the spout. A quality steel stove-top espresso maker will only take a few minutes to make a quality demitasse of espresso.

Some stove-top espresso makers also have a valve that can be used for steaming milk for cappuccinos. If your model doesn't have this value, you may use an electric device that steams milk by heating water in a chamber and forcing it through a valve by steam pressure.

If you're in the market for an electric expresso coffee, you will find that there are multiple options out there with widely ranging prices. There are also plenty of cheap ones out there that work just as well as the costly ones. The electric expresso machines have a valve for steaming milk, which makes the work easier for you.

The expresso machine you choose to buy will largely depend on your budget and your seriousness. I personally know quite a few coffee enthusiasts who are not satisfied by the cheap expresso makers and are only satisfied by powerful expresso machines.

Steaming Milk

You can skip this section if you know the proper way of steaming milk. If you're a beginner, you will need to learn how to properly steam milk using your expresso machines in order to make make great cappuccinos and lattes.

Make sure you always start off with a cold pitcher (you can place it in the fridge beforehand). A stainless-steel pitcher works best for this job. Nonfat and low-fat milk are most commonly used—although regular milk can be easily steamed once you get a little practice.

Just fill the pitcher approximately one-third to one-half with the milk. The milk will expand during the process so make sure you don't fill it over half. Put the nozzle of the steamer on the surface of the milk and turn the steam pressure all the way on.

As the steamer begins to froth the milk, lower the pitcher while the milk expands, keeping the nozzle approximately 2 inch under the surface of the milk. Be cautious not to allow the milk to boil, as it may overflow or have a slightly burnt taste.

When the froth that you've produced by steaming the milk starts to rise to the surface of the pitcher, you may turn the pressure down or take the pitcher away from the steamer, as the milk is now just on the verge of boiling.

If done right, the steamed milk will contain very small bubbles throughout the liquid, and the froth on top will have a sweet or light taste to it. You might screw up the steaming process a little the first couple of times you try it, but you will master the process if you keep at it.

Know the Ingredients

Sweeteners: Whether the recipes call for them or not, feel free to put in any kind of and any amount of sweetener to the drink. Most common sweeteners used for coffee drinks are- regular granulated sugar, honey, brown sugar etc. Just make sure you don't put in too much, as it is possible to put in sugar to a drink, but impossible to remove it. You also might want to consider enjoying these drinks without any sweetener at all.

Whipped Cream: Many of the recipes in this book will call for whipped cream. When it comes to whipped cream, fresher is always better. Put in approximately ¼ cup of whipped cream per drink. Also, whipped cream is already sweet, so it is pointless to put in additional sugar to it.

Milk: Regardless of the kind of milk a recipe calls for, feel free to use the kind of milk you like best. Whole, low-fat, and non-fat all- all kinds of milk will work in every recipe. Choose the kind of milk you personally prefer.

Chocolate Syrup: Many of the recipes in this book call for chocolate syrup. Any chocolate syrup of your choice will do the job. If you don't have any syrup, chocolate power will do the job too. Even grated chocolate will do a tremendous job.

Flavour Extracts: These are used in quite a few recipes in this book. You can easily find these in local markets and in online marketplaces. Try all brands and stick to the one you like best. You may also substitute flavour extracts with flavoured syrup. Remember that flavoured extracts are much stronger, and in general 1 tablespoon of flavored syrups is the equivalent to ¼ teaspoon extract.

Soda: Club soda, carbonated water, and sparkling water- all do the trick. A recipe might call for one of these, but feel free to substitute one with the other.

Serving Size: You don't always have to make the exact amount as the recipes as you to. Feel free to multiply or divide the amount of ingredients used by the same number.

Non-Alcoholic Coffee Recipes

Now that we are done with the basics, it is time to jump straight into the recipes!

This book contains a variety of recipes, and different recipes work best for different occasions. Feel free to find out when you like a particular recipe best.

Also, once you master the basic recipes, feel free to let your creative mind run wild, and create awesome recipes of your own!

Good luck! Have fun! Happy Drinking!

Hot Drinks Made with Brewed Coffee

Unless otherwise specified, all of the drinks in this chapter are made with freshly brewed coffee that is still hot, and should be served instantly.

Blended Banana Coffee

This drink settles if you allow it to sit for a while. So, it is best to drink it instantly.

Ingredients:

- ¼ teaspoon vanilla extract
- ½ banana, peeled, sliced, and mashed
- ½ cup heavy cream
- ½ teaspoon ground cinnamon
- 1 cup hot coffee
- 1 tablespoon butter
- 1 tablespoon confectioners' sugar

Directions:

1. Melt the butter in a saucepan over low heat.
2. Mix in the banana, cinnamon, and vanilla. Simmer for 1 to 2 minutes, stirring intermittently.
3. Turn off the heat. Place the coffee, cream, and sugar in the blender and put in the banana mixture.
4. Blend for 15 to 20 seconds, or until smooth. Serve at once.

Yield: 1 Servings

Café au Lait

This drink is highly popular, and has a mild taste of steamed milk. Feel free to vary the proportions of coffee and milk to your own personal preference.

Ingredients:

- Ground cinnamon or nutmeg, or sweetened chocolate powder (optional)
- *1/3* cup milk
- *2/3* cup coffee

Directions:

1. Pour the coffee into a cup.
2. Steam the milk and pour into the coffee, leaving a layer of froth on top.
3. Drizzle cinnamon, nutmeg, or chocolate powder on top of the foam, if you wish.

Yield: 1 Servings

Variation: To make a Café Vermont, put in 3 tablespoons maple syrup into the coffee before pouring in the steamed milk. Rest of the process is the same as above.

Café Belgique

Enjoy the mild vanilla taste of this coffee drink.

Ingredients:

- ¼ teaspoon vanilla extract

- ½ cup heavy cream
- 1 egg white
- 3 cups coffee

Directions:

1. Beat the egg white until firm.
2. Whip the cream together with the vanilla. Combine the egg white and whipped-cream mixture together and fill 4 cups one-third of the way.
3. Pour 3 cup coffee into each cup.

Yield: 4 Servings

Café Borgia

A whipped cream coffee drink with a citrus twist!

Ingredients:

- ½ cup heavy cream, whipped
- 2 cups coffee
- Grated orange peel

Directions:

1. Split the coffee into 2 cups.
2. On the top of each cup, put a large dollop of whipped cream and drizzle with grated orange peel.

Yield: 2 Servings

Café Mocha

This drink is basically chocolate + Café au Lait. Feel free to vary proportions of coffee and milk according to your own personal preference.

Ingredients:

- 1/3 cup milk
- 2 tablespoons chocolate syrup
- 2/3 cup coffee
- Sweetened chocolate powder (optional)

Directions:

1. Pour the coffee into a cup.
2. Mix the chocolate syrup into the coffee.
3. Steam the milk until hot and foamy, then pour into the coffee, leaving a layer of froth on top.
4. Drizzle chocolate powder on top, if you wish.

Yield: 1 Servings

Variations: To make a Café Mocha Mint, mix 1/8 teaspoon mint extract into the coffee together with the chocolate syrup. Rest of the process is the same as above and decorate with a fresh mint sprig, if you wish.

To make a Mandarin Mocha, mix 1/8 teaspoon orange extract into the coffee together with the chocolate syrup. Rest of the process is the same as above.

Café Vanilla

This recipe flavoured with the vanilla bean tastes a little like an expresso.

Ingredients:

- ¼ vanilla bean
- ½ cup milk
- ¾ cup coffee
- 1 teaspoon brown sugar
- Ground cinnamon or nutmeg

Directions:

1. Cut the vanilla bean along the length and place it with the milk and brown sugar in a saucepan.
2. Bring to a boil, stirring intermittently.
3. Turn off the heat, cover, and allow it to stand for a few minutes.
4. Remove the vanilla bean and pulse the milk mixture in a blender for approximately 30 seconds, or until it becomes foamy.
5. Put into the hot coffee and put on top the cinnamon or nutmeg.

Chocolate Cream Coffee

A great drink to keep warm on a cold winter evening.

Ingredients:

- ¼ cup heavy cream
- 1 cup coffee

- 3 tablespoons chocolate syrup
- Grated orange peel
- Ground cinnamon
- Sweetened chocolate powder

Directions:

1. Whip all excluding 1 tablespoon of the cream.
2. Mix the remaining tablespoon of cream and the chocolate syrup in a saucepan over low heat until completely blended.
3. Pour in the coffee slowly, stirring the mixture as you do so.
4. Transfer to a mug and put on top the whipped cream and cinnamon, chocolate powder, and grated orange peel.

Yield: 2 Servings

Chocolate-Vanilla Coffee

Chocolate and vanilla are a timeless combo. You can enjoy this drink hot or cold.

Ingredients:

- ¼ cup heavy cream, whipped
- ¼ teaspoon vanilla extract
- 1 cup coffee
- 1 tablespoon chocolate syrup

Directions:

1. Mix the chocolate syrup and vanilla into the hot coffee.
2. Put on top the whipped cream.

Yield: 1 Servings

Cinnamon - Vanilla Coffee

Vanilla and Cinnamon go well together in coffee drinks.

Ingredients:

- ¼ vanilla bean, sliced
- ½ cup heavy cream
- 1 cinnamon stick
- 1 tablespoon or more brown sugar
- 1½ cups coffee

Directions:

1. Before brewing the coffee, cut the vanilla bean along the length and place it with the cinnamon stick in the bottom of the coffee maker carafe.
2. While the coffee is brewing, whip the cream and brown sugar together.
3. Pour the coffee into 2 cups and put on top the the whipped cream mixture. Put in extra brown sugar to taste, if you wish.

Yield: 2 Servings

Coffee Grog

A rich-tasting coffee drink.

Ingredients:

- 1 cup brown sugar
- *1/8* teaspoon ground allspice
- *1/8* teaspoon ground cinnamon
- *1/8* teaspoon ground cloves
- *1/8* teaspoon ground nutmeg
- 1½ cups heavy cream or half-and-half
- 1½ teaspoons rum extract (optional)
- 12 small strips of lemon peel
- 12 small strips of orange peel
- 2 tablespoons butter
- 9 cups coffee

Directions:

1. Melt the butter in a saucepan over low heat.
2. Mix in the brown sugar, allspice, cinnamon, nutmeg, and cloves, and let the mixture cool. Store in an airtight container in the fridge.
3. To serve, mix in each cup 1 teaspoon of the butter mixture, 2 tablespoons cream, 1 strip orange peel, and 1 strip lemon peel. Put in 6 ounces of hot coffee and stir. You may also put in teaspoon rum extract to each cup of grog, if you wish.

Yield: 12 Servings

Variation: Don't use the allspice and cinnamon and double the amount of ground nutmeg and cloves. Rest of the process is the same as above.

Hawaiian Coffee

A delicious recipe that is a hit in every weather.

Ingredients:

- ½ cup coffee
- ½ cup milk
- ½ cup sweetened shredded coconut

Directions:

1. Preheat the oven to 350°F. Place the milk and coconut in a saucepan and warm over low heat for 2 to 3 minutes, stirring intermittently.
2. Strain the milk and place the coconut on a baking sheet in the oven until it turns brown, approximately 8 to 10 minutes.
3. Put in the milk to the hot coffee and put on top the the browned coconut.

Yield: 1 Servings

New Orleans Coffee

If you like the earthy taste of chicory, this recipe is for you!

Ingredients:

- 1 cup coffee, with 25 percent ground chicory

- 1 cup steamed milk
- Ground cinnamon

Directions:

1. Pour the coffee into two cups.
2. Put in steamed milk evenly to both and top off each cup with some froth from the steamed milk.
3. Drizzle cinnamon on top.

Yield: 2 Servings

Spiced Coffee

Spices go great with coffee. Feel free to try your favourite spices in this recipe instead of the ones I've mentioned!

Ingredients:

- ¼ teaspoon whole allspice
- ½ cup heavy cream, whipped
- 1 cinnamon stick
- 1½ cups coffee
- 2 whole cloves
- Ground cinnamon
- White or brown sugar, to taste

Directions:

1. Pour the coffee over the cinnamon stick, cloves, and allspice in a saucepan and simmer over low heat for 5 to 7 minutes.

2. Strain into cups, put on top the whipped cream, and drizzle with cinnamon. Put in white or brown sugar to taste.

Yield: 2 Servings

Variation: Don't use the cinnamon stick and allspice and substitute 2 strips each of orange and lemon peel; use 10 cloves instead of 2. Rest of the process is the same as above.

Spiced Coffee Cider
A spicy fruity coffee!

Ingredients:

- ½ cup apple juice
- ½ cup coffee
- 1 cinnamon stick
- 1 teaspoon brown sugar
- 1 thin cut of orange, including rind
- 1/8 teaspoon ground allspice
- *1/8* teaspoon ground cloves
- Ground cinnamon (optional)

Directions:

1. Mix all the ingredients excluding cinnamon together in a saucepan and simmer over low heat for 3 to 4 minutes, stirring intermittently.
2. Strain into a mug and drizzle with cinnamon, if you wish.

Yield: 1 Servings

Spiced Cream Coffee

Chocolate and spicy whipped cream go so well together!

Ingredients:

- ¼ teaspoon ground nutmeg
- ½ cup heavy cream
- ¾ teaspoon ground cinnamon
- 1 tablespoon sugar
- 1½ cups coffee
- 2 teaspoons chocolate syrup

Directions:

1. Mix 1/4 teaspoon of the cinnamon and the nutmeg and sugar into the cream and whip.
2. Split the coffee into two 6-ounce portions and mix 1 teaspoon chocolate syrup and 1/4 teaspoon cinnamon into each cup.
3. Put on top the spiced whipped cream.

Yield: 2 Servings

Turkish Coffee

A middle eastern favourite!

Ingredients:

- 1 tablespoon extremely fine ground or powdered coffee

- 1½ to 2 teaspoons sugar (optional)
- 2 ounces cold water

Directions:

1. In a jezve, mix all the ingredients together.
2. Heat on low setting and gradually bring this mixture to a boil without stirring.
3. When it starts to boil, turn off the heat and pour into a demitasse.
4. Allow the grounds to settle before drinking, or put in a tiny splash of cold water to help settle the grounds.

Yield: 1 Servings

Variations: To make a frothier drink, allow the coffee to froth up, turn off the heat, and spoon the top froth into your cup. Turn the heat back on and repeat this process two more times, then pour the liquid into the cup. If you wish to add more taste to this recipe, put in 1/8 teaspoon ground cardamom, cinnamon, nutmeg, or cloves to the ground coffee before brewing. To make a rich, creamy drink, use milk instead of water.

Viennese Coffee

Looking for a delicious coffee recipe with a whipped cream topping? Look no further!

Ingredients:

- ½ cup heavy cream, whipped

- 2 cups coffee, preferably Viennese or other dark roast
- Ground cinnamon, nutmeg, or cloves

Directions:

1. Pour the coffee into 2 cups.
2. On the top of each cup, put a large dollop of whipped cream and drizzle with cinnamon, nutmeg, or cloves.

Yield: 2 Servings

Hot Drinks Made with Espresso

Expresso is easily one of the most popular coffee recipes around the world. In this section I will teach you to make a few basic expresso coffee recipes. These recipes form the base for many of the recipes that follow in this book. The single expresso and the double expresso are two of the recipes in this section that form the basic ingredient in many of the recipes in the following sections of this book, so make sure you got those down.

Single Espresso:

A single espresso consists of approximately 1½ ounces of extremely strong-tasting coffee. It is made using a dark-roasted bean, using either a stove-top espresso maker or an electric machine. It serves as the basis for many exotic coffee drinks, both hot and cold, and has numerous variations of its own. Put in almond, rum, brandy, mint, or vanilla extract to taste, if you wish. You may also drizzle spices such as ground cinnamon and cardamom onto your espresso.

Double Espresso:

Use twice the amount of water and coffee grounds as you would for a single espresso.

Ristretto:

Use the same amount of grounds as for a single espresso, but stop the flow of water at approximately 1 ounce. This is also called as a "short" espresso.

Espresso Romano:

A single espresso served with a small cut of lemon peel.

Espresso Anise:

A single espresso with 1/8 teaspoon anise extract added. For an Espresso Anise Royale, put whipped cream on top.

Americano:

A single espresso with hot water added to taste (usually approximately 1 cup).

Red Eye:

A single espresso added to 1 cup brewed coffee.

Macchiato:

A single espresso with a dollop of froth from steamed milk (1 to 2 tablespoons) on top.

Espresso con Panna:

A single espresso topped with whipped cream.

Espresso Borgia:

A single espresso topped with whipped cream (or froth from steamed milk) and grated orange peel.

Espresso Grog:

Prepare a grog mixture as described in the recipe for Coffee Grog. For each cup of Espresso Grog, place 1 teaspoon of the grog mixture in the bottom of the cup, together with 1 tablespoon heavy cream (or halfand-half), 1 small strip orange peel, and 1 small strip lemon peel. Put in a single espresso to each of these cups and mix in the grog mixture thoroughly. You may also put in a tiny amount (less than 1/8 teaspoon) of rum extract to each cup of grog, if you wish.

Makes 12 servings

Cappuccino:

This drink consists of one-third espresso (a single) and one-third steamed milk, and is topped with one-third froth from the steamed milk. Drizzle ground cinnamon, nutmeg, or sweetened chocolate powder on top, if you wish. You may also put in almond, rum, brandy, mint, or vanilla extract to taste. To make a Double Cappuccino, use a double espresso instead of a single.

Cappuccino Royale:

A cappuccino topped with whipped cream, and soemtimes with almond, rum, brandy, mint, or vanilla extract added to taste. Decorate with a thin wafer.

Butterscotch Cappuccino:

Put in butterscotch syrup to a cappuccino to taste. To make a Butterscotch Latte, do the same thing with a Caffè Latte.

Caffè Latte:

This drink consists of a single espresso with the remainder of the glass filled up with steamed milk, and is topped off with a thin layer of froth from the steamed milk. Drizzle ground cinnamon, nutmeg, or sweetened chocolate powder on top, if you wish. You may also put in almond, rum, brandy, mint, or vanilla extract to taste. To make a Double Caffè Latte, use a double espresso instead of a single.

Latte Macchiato:

Pour steamed milk, topped with froth from the steamed milk into a glass; then softly pour a single espresso into the glass. The espresso will gradually drip to the bottom.

Mochaccino:

This drink consists of one-third espresso (a single), one-third steamed chocolate milk, and one-third froth from the steamed chocolate milk for topping. (You may also make this drink by stirring chocolate syrup into the espresso, adding one-third steamed milk, and topping it off with one-third froth from the steamed milk.) Put on top the whipped cream and sweetened chocolate powder, if you wish. To make a Double Mochaccino, use a double espresso instead of a single.

Mocha Latte:

This drink consists of a single espresso with the remainder of the glass filled up with steamed chocolate milk, and topped off with a thin layer of froth from the steamed chocolate milk. (You may also make this drink by stirring chocolate syrup into the espresso, filling up the remainder of the glass with steamed milk, and topping it off with a thin layer of froth from the steamed milk.) Put on top the whipped cream and sweetened chocolate powder, if you wish. To make a Double Mocha Latte, use a double espresso instead of a single.

Spiced Chocolate Espresso
Spice, chocolate, and Espresso in one drink!

Ingredients:

- ¼ teaspoon ground cinnamon
- 1/8 teaspoon ground nutmeg
- 2 double espressos
- 2 ounces heavy cream or half-and-half
- 2 teaspoons chocolate syrup Whipped cream
- 2 teaspoons sugar

Directions:

1. Combine all the ingredients excluding the chocolate syrup and whipped cream in a pitcher and steam until hot and foamy.
2. Transfer to 2 mugs, put in 1 teaspoon chocolate syrup to each, and stir.
3. Put on top the whipped cream.

Yield: 2 Servings

Cold Drinks Made with Brewed Coffee

Unless otherwise specified, all of the drinks in this section are made with cold coffee. In order to account for the dilution factor of ice cubes, you should brew coffee using one-and-a-half times to twice the normal amount of ground coffee per cup. Then store the coffee in an airtight container in the fridge. You can also use coffee ice cubes, as I taught you previously.

Banana Coffee Blend

Serve this drink as soon as possible after its made!

Ingredients:

- 1 banana, peeled and sliced
- 1 cup coffee
- 1 cup milk

- 1 tablespoon confectioners' sugar

Directions:

1. Combine all the ingredients together in a blender.
2. Pulse for 15 to 20 seconds, or until smooth.

Yield: 1 Servings

Blended Chocolate Coffee

A light coffee drink with the goodness of chocolate!

Ingredients:

- ½ cup coffee
- 1 tablespoon sugar
- 2 cups milk
- 2 tablespoons chocolate syrup
- Ice cubes
- Sweetened chocolate powder (optional)
- Whipped cream (optional)

Directions:

1. Combine the coffee, milk, chocolate syrup, and sugar in a blender for 15 to 20 seconds, or until foamy.
2. Pour over ice in 2 tall glasses and put on top the whipped cream and chocolate powder, if you wish.

Yield: 2 Servings

Blended Honey Coffee

A nice and easy coffee recipe great for those rushed mornings!

Ingredients:

- ¾ cup coffee
- ¾ cup milk
- 1 tablespoon honey

Directions:

1. Combine all the ingredients together in a blender.
2. Pulse for 10 to 15 seconds.

Yield: 1 Servings

Blended Vanilla Coffee

A light coffee drink with the goodness of vanilla!

Ingredients:

- ½ cup coffee
- ½ teaspoon vanilla extract
- 1 cup milk
- 1 tablespoon sugar
- Ground cinnamon (optional)
- Ice cubes

Directions:

1. Combine all the ingredients excluding the ice and cinnamon in a blender for 15 to 20 seconds, or until foamy.

2. Pour over ice in a tall glass, and put on top the a dash of cinnamon, if you wish.

Yield: 1 Servings

Butterscotch Coffee Shake

Who doesn't love butterscotch?

Ingredients:

- 1 scoop vanilla (or coffee) ice cream
- 2 tablespoons butterscotch syrup
- 2¼ tablespoons heavy cream
- 5 ounces coffee

Directions:

1. Combine all the ingredients together in a blender.
2. Pulse for 15 to 20 seconds, or until smooth.

Yield: 1 Servings

Chocolate-Coffee Crush

One of the most popular drinks in coffee shops today!

Ingredients:

- ½ cup crushed ice
- ½ cup milk
- ¾ cup coffee
- 2 tablespoons chocolate syrup
- Sugar, to taste

- Sweetened chocolate powder (optional)
- Whipped cream (optional)

Directions:

1. Combine all the ingredients excluding the whipped cream and chocolate powder in a blender for 15 to 20 seconds, or until smooth.
2. Transfer to a tall glass and put on top the whipped cream and chocolate powder, if you wish.

Yield: 1 Servings

Variations: To make a Vanilla-Coffee Crush, omit the chocolate syrup and substitute i teaspoon vanilla extract. Rest of the process is the same as above. To make a Creamy Coffee Crush, simply omit the chocolate syrup.

Coffee Crush

This is best consumed instantly.

Ingredients:

- ¾ cup coffee
- 1¼ cups crushed ice
- Ice cubes
- Sugar to taste
- Sweetened chocolate powder, ground cinnamon or nutmeg (optional)
- Whipped cream (optional)

Directions:

1. Combine the coffee, crushed ice, and sugar in a blender for 15 to 20 seconds, or until foamy.
2. Pour over ice, put on top the whipped cream, and drizzle with chocolate powder, cinnamon, or nutmeg, if you wish.

Yield: 2 Servings

Honey Iced Coffee

A sweet and smooth coffee recipe with the flavour of honey! Add the honey to the freshly brewed hot coffee to have an easier time mixing.

Ingredients:

- 1 cup freshly brewed coffee
- Ground cinnamon and nutmeg
- Honey, to taste
- Ice cubes
- Whipped cream (optional)

Directions:

1. Mix the honey into the coffee to taste.
2. Put in ice and put on top the whipped cream,
3. if you wish. Drizzle with cinnamon and nutmeg.

Yield: 1 Servings

Hot Coffee Float

A recipe with the ultimate bland of ice-creams!

Ingredients:

- ¼ cup heavy cream, whipped
- ¾ cup freshly brewed coffee, still piping hot
- 1 scoop each vanilla, chocolate, and coffee ice cream

Directions:

1. Place the scoops of ice cream in a tall glass and put in the coffee.
2. Put on top the the whipped cream.

Yield: 1 Servings

Iced Almond Coffee

A great drink to satisfy your sweet tooth!

Ingredients:

- 1 cup heavy cream, whipped
- 1 teaspoon almond extract Ice cubes
- 2 cups half-and-half
- 2 tablespoons sugar
- 4 cups coffee
- 4 tablespoons sweetened condensed milk
- Sliced almonds, for garnish

Directions:

1. Combine the coffee, half-and-half, condensed milk, sugar, and almond extract in a pitcher.
2. Pour over ice in 4 glasses or mugs.

3. Top each portion with whipped cream and decorate with a few slices of almond.

Yield: 4 Servings

Iced Café au Lait

The froth on top of this drink provides a subtle taste through which to drink your coffee.

Ingredients:

- Ice cubes
- *1/3* cup milk
- *2/3* cup coffee

Directions:

1. Fill a glass with ice.
2. Pour in the coffee.
3. Steam the milk and pour into the glass, leaving a layer of froth on top.

Yield: 1 Servings

Iced Cardamom Coffee

Another blast from the middle east!

Ingredients:

- ½ teaspoon cardamom seeds
- 2 cups water
- 4 tablespoons coffee grounds

- Ice cubes
- Lemon or pineapple slices, or maraschino cherries, for garnish
- Sugar, to taste

Directions:

1. Boil the cardamom seeds in the water for approximately 5 minutes.
2. Strain and use this water to brew your coffee.
3. Pour the coffee over ice and sweeten with sugar to taste.
4. Decorate with slices of lemon or pineapple or with maraschino cherries.

Yield: 2 Servings

Iced Coffee Bitters

A cool recipe with a tangy taste!

Ingredients:

- ½ teaspoon bitters
- 1 teaspoon vanilla extract
- 4 tablespoons sugar
- 4½ cups coffee
- Ice cubes
- Whipped cream or halfand-half (optional)

Directions:

1. Combine the bitters, vanilla, and sugar together with 2 tablespoons of the coffee until the mixture is a thick syrup.
2. Put in 2½ teaspoons of this mixture to every 6 ounces of coffee. Serve over ice.
3. Put on top the whipped cream or lightly pour 2 tablespoons half-and-half onto the top of each drink, if you wish.

Yield: 6 Servings

Iced Maple Coffee

The perfect recipe for all maple syrup lovers out there!

Ingredients:

- ¼ cup heavy cream, whipped
- 1 cup freshly brewed coffee
- 3 tablespoons maple syrup
- Ice cubes

Directions:

1. Mix the maple syrup into the coffee and pour over ice.
2. Put on top the whipped cream.

Yield: 1 Servings

Iced Mint Coffee

A cold minty caffeinated drink feels great on a hot summer afternoon.

Ingredients:

- ½ cup coffee
- 1 tablespoon heavy cream, or ¼ cup milk or half and-half
- *1/8* teaspoon mint extract
- Fresh mint sprig, for garnish
- Ice cubes

Directions:

1. Blend together the coffee, mint, and cream.
2. Pour over ice. Decorate with a fresh mint sprig.

Yield: 1 Servings

Variations: Don't use the cream and proceed as directed above, or omit the mint extract and mint sprig and substitute 1/8 teaspoon almond, rum, brandy, or vanilla extract.

Spiced Iced Coffee Combo One

This is a recipe I personally like. Feel free to replace the spices with ones you personally like.

Ingredients:

- 1 cinnamon stick
- *1/8* teaspoon ground allspice

- 1½ cups freshly brewed coffee
- 1½ tablespoons sugar
- 3 whole cloves
- Ice cubes
- Whipped cream (optional)

Directions:

1. Place all the ingredients excluding the ice and whipped cream in a saucepan and warm over low heat.
2. Mix until the sugar is dissolved. Allow the mixture to cool to room temperature, approximately 30 minutes.
3. Remove the cinnamon stick and cloves, and pour over ice.
4. Put on top the whipped cream, if you wish.

Yield: 2 Servings

Spiced Iced Combo Two

A great recipe to make ahead of time.

Ingredients:

- ¼ teaspoon cardamom seeds
- ¼ teaspoon whole allspice
- 2 cinnamon sticks
- 4 cups freshly brewed coffee
- 4 whole cloves
- Brown sugar (optional)
- Ice cubes

- Milk (optional)

Directions:

1. Place the cinnamon sticks, cloves, allspice, and cardamom seeds at the bottom of a container, and pour coffee over the spices.
2. Allow the mixture to cool to room temperature, approximately 30 minutes. Strain into a new container and store in the fridge.
3. When ready to serve, pour over ice and put in milk and brown sugar, if you wish.

Yield: 4 to 6 Servings

Variation: Don't use the four spices and put in 4 strips each of orange and lemon peel, and 8 cloves. Rest of the process is the same as above.

Strawberry Delight

Feel free to swap out the strawberry for a fruit of your choice!

Ingredients:

- ¼ teaspoon almond extract
- ½ cup coffee
- ½ cup heavy cream
- 4 strawberries
- Additional strawberries, for garnish
- Confectioners' sugar, to taste
- Ice cubes (optional)

Directions:

1. Whip ¼ cup of the cream and set aside.
2. Combine the coffee, remaining cream, 4 strawberries, almond extract, and sugar in a blender for 15 to 20 seconds, or until smooth.
3. Put on top the the whipped cream and decorate with fresh strawberries. (You may also pour this drink over ice, if you wish.)

Yield: 1 Servings

Variations: To make a Raspberry Delight, omit the strawberries and substitute 12 raspberries. Rest of the process is the same as above. Decorate with fresh raspberries. To make a Kiwi Delight, substitute 1 kiwi fruit, peeled and sliced, for the strawberries. Rest of the process is the same as above. Decorate with a few slices of kiwi.

Tropical Coffee Delight

You will love this drink on a warm summer day.

Ingredients:

- ¼ cup papaya nectar
- ½ cup coffee
- ½ kiwi fruit, peeled and sliced
- 1 scoop vanilla ice cream
- 1 tablespoon cream of coconut
- 3–4 tablespoons heavy cream (optional)

Directions:

1. Combine the coffee, papaya, ¼ kiwi, coconut, and ice cream in a blender for 15 to 20 seconds, or until smooth.
2. Decorate with the remaining kiwi and pour the heavy cream lightly on top, if you wish.

Yield: 1 Servings

Vani-Chococolate Coffee Shake

Cinnamon makes everything taste better!

Ingredients:

- ½ cup coffee
- 1 tablespoon chocolate syrup
- *1/8* teaspoon ground cinnamon
- 2 scoops vanilla ice cream
- Whipped cream (optional)

Directions:

1. Combine all the ingredients excluding the whipped cream in a blender for 15 to 20 seconds, or until smooth.
2. Put on top the whipped cream, if you wish.

Yield: 1 Servings

Variations: To make a Chocolate Coffee Shake, omit the vanilla ice cream and cinnamon and substitute 2 scoops of chocolate ice cream and 1/8 teaspoon ground nutmeg. Rest of the process is the same as above. To make a Coffee

Coffee Shake, substitute 2 scoops of coffee ice cream for the vanilla ice cream and cinnamon.

Vanilla-Banana Coffee Shake

An insanely delicious and rich-tasting coffee shake!

Ingredients:

- ½ cup coffee
- 2 scoops vanilla ice cream
- Whipped cream (optional)
- 1/3 banana, peeled and sliced
- 1/8 teaspoon almond extract
- 1/8 teaspoon ground cinnamon

Directions:

1. Combine all the ingredients excluding the whipped cream in a blender for 15 to 20 seconds, or until smooth.
2. Put on top the whipped cream, if you wish.

Yield: 1 Servings

Vanilla-Rum Coffee Shake

A great drink for all those who love the flavour of rum extract!

Ingredients:

- ½ teaspoon rum extract
- 1½ cups coffee

- 2 scoops vanilla ice cream
- Ice cubes

Directions:

1. Combine all the ingredients excluding the ice in a blender.
2. Pulse for 15 to 20 seconds, or until smooth.
3. Pour over ice in tall glasses.

Yield: 2 Servings

Yogurt Coffee Shake

I love this recipe on a hot afternoon.

Ingredients:

- ¼ teaspoon vanilla extract
- ½ cup coffee
- 1 cup vanilla yogurt
- 1 teaspoon confectioners' sugar

Directions:

1. Combine all the ingredients together in a blender.
2. Pulse for 15 to 20 seconds, or until smooth.

Yield: 1 Servings

Cold Drinks Made with Espresso

All recipes in this section will call for a basic espresso drink. You will particularly need to know how to make those single and double espressos. Most recipes don't require much espresso, so you might not need to cool the drink even after adding the espresso.

If you with to make these drinks in large batches, it is usually a good idea to prepare the espresso in advance, and store it in an airtight container in a fridge. This will also reduce the amount of ice and cooling you will need after you've prepared the drink.

However, you should know that the flavour of espresso declines with time, so time the preparation of espresso. Don't prepare it too early.

Below are a few basic recipes you can make with cold espresso. Make sure to use these as a base in your own recipes!

Iced Espresso:

A single or double espresso poured over ice cubes. Decorate with a small cut of lemon peel, if you wish.

Iced Americano:

Put in hot water to a single espresso to taste, then pour over ice cubes.

Iced Macchiato:

An iced espresso with a dollop of froth from steamed milk (1 to 2 tablespoons) on top.

Iced Espresso con Panna:

An iced espresso topped with whipped cream.

Iced Maple Espresso:

Mix 2 tablespoons maple syrup into a single espresso. Pour over ice cubes and put on top the whipped cream, if you wish. To make a Double Iced Maple Espresso, use twice the amount of maple syrup and espresso as for a single.

Iced Cappuccino:

This drink consists of one-third espresso (a single), one-third cold milk, and one-third froth topping from steamed milk, over ice cubes. Drizzle ground cinnamon or nutmeg or sweetened chocolate powder on top, and decorate with a fresh mint leaf, if you wish. You may also put in almond, rum, brandy, mint, or vanilla extract to taste. To make a Double Iced Cappuccino, use a double espresso instead of a single.

Iced Cappuccino Royale:

An Iced Cappuccino topped with whipped cream and garnished with a thin wafer. Put in almond, rum, brandy, mint, or vanilla extract to taste, if you wish.

Iced Caffè Latte:

Pour a single espresso over ice cubes in a tall glass. Fill the rest of glass with cold milk and put on top the a thin layer of froth from steamed milk. Drizzle ground cinnamon or nutmeg or sweetened chocolate powder on top, and decorate with a mint leaf, if you wish. You may also put in almond, rum, brandy, mint, or vanilla extract to taste. To make a Double Iced Caffè Latte, use a double espresso instead of a single.

Iced Mochaccino:

This drink consists of one-third espresso (a single), one-third cold chocolate milk, and one-third froth topping from steamed chocolate (or regular) milk, over ice cubes. Put on top the whipped cream and sweetened chocolate powder, if you wish. To make a Double Iced Mochaccino, use a double espresso instead of a single.

Iced Mocha Latte:

Pour a single espresso over ice cubes in a tall glass. Fill the rest of glass with cold chocolate milk. Put in a thin layer of froth from steamed chocolate (or regular) milk and put on top the whipped cream and sweetened chocolate powder, if you wish. To make a Double Iced Mocha Latte, use a double espresso instead of a single.

Blended Honey Latte

An easy drink that tastes great!

Ingredients:

- Single espresso
- ¾ cup milk
- 1 teaspoon honey

Directions:

1. Combine all the ingredients together in a blender.
2. Pulse for 10 to 15 seconds.

Yield: 1 Servings

Chocolate Espresso Crush

Use Ice cream instead of crushed ice in this recipe to make it taste even sweeter and richer!

Ingredients:

- Double espresso
- ¼ cup milk
- ½ cup crushed ice
- 2 tablespoons chocolate syrup
- Sugar, to taste

Page | 56

- Sweetened chocolate powder (optional)
- Whipped cream (optional)

Directions:

1. Combine all the ingredients excluding the whipped cream and chocolate powder in a blender.
2. Pulse for 15 to 20 seconds, or until smooth.
3. Put on top the whipped cream and chocolate powder, if you wish.

Yield: 1 Servings

Variations: To make a Vanilla Espresso Crush, substitute 1 teaspoon vanilla extract for the chocolate syrup. To make a Creamy Espresso Crush, omit the chocolate syrup.

Espresso Crush

A delicious coffee drink made rich with whipped cream!

Ingredients:

- Double espresso
- ½ cup crushed ice Sugar, to taste Ice cubes
- Sweetened chocolate powder, ground cinnamon or nutmeg (optional)
- Whipped cream (optional)

Directions:

1. Combine the espresso, crushed ice, and sugar in a blender for 15 to 20 seconds, or until foamy.

2. Pour over ice. If desired, put on top the whipped cream and drizzle with chocolate powder, cinnamon, or nutmeg.

Yield: 1 Servings

Espresso Float

A sweet and satisfying drink that quenches hunger.

Ingredients:

- Double espresso
- ¼ cup heavy cream, whipped
- ¼ cup milk
- 1 cinnamon stick, for garnish
- 2 scoops vanilla ice cream
- Sweetened chocolate powder

Directions:

1. Pour the espresso into a tall glass.
2. Put in the milk and ice cream and put on top the whipped cream and chocolate powder.
3. Decorate with the cinnamon stick.

Yield: 1 Servings

Variations: Instead of vanilla ice cream, use 2 scoops of chocolate or coffee ice cream. Rest of the process is the same as above. To make a Cappuccino Float, use a hot or iced cappuccino with 1 scoop of vanilla ice cream. To make a Chocoloccino, use chocolate ice cream. To make a

Mochaccino Float, use a hot or iced mochaccino with 1 scoop of vanilla ice cream.

Espresso Ice Cream Soda

A highly satisfying coffee drink!

Ingredients:

- Single espresso
- ½ cup carbonated water (or cola)
- 1 ounce half-and-half (optional)
- 1 scoop vanilla ice cream
- Ice cubes

Directions:

1. Pour espresso and half-and-half, if you wish, over ice.
2. Put in carbonated water and ice cream.

Yield: 1 Servings

Espresso Soda

A super strong and refreshing drink!

Ingredients:

- Single espresso
- ½ cup carbonated water (or cola)
- Ice cubes
- Lemon, orange, or lime peel, for garnish

Directions:

1. Pour the espresso over ice.
2. Put in carbonated water and decorate with a small piece of lemon, orange, or lime peel.

Yield: 1 Servings

Variation: To make a Double Espresso Soda, use double the amount of espresso and carbonated water (or cola).

Rum Espresso Soda

Flavour of rum always goes great with coffee!

Ingredients:

- Single espresso
- ¼ cup heavy cream
- ¼ teaspoon rum extract
- ½ cup carbonated water
- Ice cubes
- Sugar, to taste

Directions:

1. Combine the espresso, cream, and rum together and pour over ice.
2. Put in the carbonated water and sugar to taste.

Yield: 1 Servings

Tropical Espresso Delight

A great recipe to cool you down!

Ingredients:

- Single espresso
- ¼ kiwi fruit, peeled and sliced
- ½ scoop vanilla ice cream
- 1 teaspoon cream of coconut
- 1 to 2 tablespoons heavy cream (optional)
- *1/8* cup papaya nectar

Directions:

1. Combine the espresso, papaya, coconut, 1/8 kiwi, and the ice cream in a blender for 15 to 20 seconds, or until smooth.
2. Decorate with the remaining kiwi and pour the cream lightly on top, if you wish.

Yield: 1 Servings

Exotic Coffee Drinks with Liquor

No book about exotic coffee recipe could ever be complete without at least a few drinks with the goodness of alcohol. Today, the most popular alcoholic drinks used in coffee drinks are- rum, whiskey, brandy, cognac, crème de menthe, crème de cacao, amaretto, anisette, Irish cream, Kahlúa and Tia Maria, Cointreau and Grand

Marnier, Galliano and Frangelico. You could use these alcoholic drinks as they are, or you could pour a combination of these you're your coffee drinks.

Small amounts of other drinks like kirsch, vodka, tequila, gin, curaçao, crème de banana, cherry liqueur, calvados, Benedictine, Tuaca, Strega, Sambuca, or Drambuie also go well with coffee drinks. Feel free to experiment and use drinks and combinations you personally love best!

Hot Drinks Made With Brewed Coffee

These drinks are made with freshly brewed coffee and should be served instantly.

Café Brûlot

A great drink when you're feeling cold.

Ingredients:

- ¾ cup coffee
- 1 cinnamon stick
- 1 strip lemon peel
- 1 strip orange peel
- 1 teaspoon Cointreau or Grand Marnier (optional)
- 1 teaspoon white or brown sugar
- 1½ ounces brandy or cognac

- 2 whole cloves

Directions:

1. Place all the ingredients excluding the coffee and Cointreau in a saucepan and warm over low heat for 1 to 2 minutes, stirring intermittently.
2. Pour in the coffee and mix into the mixture. Strain into a cup. Put in the Cointreau, if you wish.

Yield: 1 Servings

Crème de Cacao Coffee

A sweet and refreshing drink.

Ingredients:

- ¼ cup heavy cream, whipped
- ¼ teaspoon Frangelico
- ¾ cup coffee
- 1½ tablespoons Bailey's Original Irish Cream
- 1½ tablespoons crème de cacao
- Ground cinnamon

Directions:

1. Combine the Bailey's, crème de cacao, and Frangelico in a glass and put in the coffee.
2. Put on top the whipped cream and a dash of cinnamon.

Yield: 1 Servings

Variation: Substitute 1 teaspoon amaretto for the Frangelico. Rest of the process is the same as above.

Irish Coffee

A timeless classic, loved my everyone!

Ingredients:

- ¼ cup heavy cream, lightly whipped
- 1 teaspoon sugar
- 2 tablespoons Irish whiskey
- 2/3 cup coffee

Directions:

1. Place the sugar and whiskey in glass, put in the coffee, and stir.
2. Put on top the lightly whipped cream.

Yield: 1 Servings

Kahlúa — Crème de Menthe Coffee

A great coffee drink that uses the delicious Kahlúa.

Ingredients:

- ¼ cup heavy cream, whipped
- ¾ cup coffee
- 2 tablespoons crème de menthe
- 2 tablespoons Kahlúa
- Sweetened chocolate powder

Directions:

1. Combine the Kahlúa and crème de menthe in a glass.
2. Pour in the coffee and put on top the whipped cream and chocolate powder.

Yield: 1 Servings

Variation: To make a Kahlúa-Crème de Cacao Coffee, omit the crème de menthe and substitute 2 tablespoons crème de cacao. Rest of the process is the same as above.

Kahlúa — Grand Marnier Coffee

A great drink if you love the taste of orange.

Ingredients:

*   ¼ cup heavy cream, whipped
*   ¾ cup coffee
*   1½ teaspoons Bailey's Original Irish Cream
*   1½ teaspoons Frangelico
*   1½ teaspoons Grand Marnier
*   1½ teaspoons Kahlúa
*   Grated orange peel, for garnish

Directions:

1. Combine the Kahlúa, Grand Marnier, Bailey's, and Frangelico in a glass.
2. Pour in the coffee and put on top the whipped cream.
3. Decorate with orange peel.

Yield: 1 Servings

Kioki Coffee

This coffee recipe tasted nothing like any other coffee drink you've tasted before.

Ingredients:

- ¼ cup heavy cream, whipped
- 1 cup coffee
- 1 tablespoon brandy
- 2 tablespoons Kahlúa

Directions:

1. Pour the Kahlúa and brandy into a mug.
2. Pour in the coffee and put on top the whipped cream.

Yield: 1 Servings

Variation: Instead of 2 tablespoons Kahlúa, use 1 tablespoon Kahlúa and 1 tablespoon crème de cacao. Rest of the process is the same as above.

Hot Drinks Made with Espresso

The following drinks are made with fresh espresso that is still hot. Serve instantly.

Espresso Anisette:

A single espresso with 1 teaspoon of anisette added. Serve with a small cut of lemon peel.

Espresso Galliano:

A single espresso with 1 teaspoon of Galliano added. Serve with a small cut of lemon peel.

Espresso Kahlúa:

A single espresso with 1 teaspoon of Kahlúa added and topped with froth from steamed milk.

Espresso Rum:

A single espresso with 1 teaspoon of rum added. Put on top the whipped cream and a dash of ground cinnamon.

Espresso Whiskey:

A single espresso with 2 teaspoon of Irish whiskey added. Put on top the whipped cream.

Caffè Corretto:

A single espresso with 1 teaspoon of grappa added.

Amaretto-Rum Cappuccino

The taste of almond-cream is super satisfying!

Ingredients:

- Single espresso
- ¼ cup heavy cream, whipped
- 1½ teaspoons amaretto
- 1½ teaspoons crème de cacao
- 1½ teaspoons rum
- 3 ounces milk, steamed
- Sliced almonds, for garnish

Directions:

1. Combine the espresso, amaretto, rum, and crème de cacao in a glass.
2. Put in 1½ ounces steamed milk and 1½ ounces milk foam.
3. Put on top the whipped cream and decorate with almond slices.

Yield: 1 Servings

Brandy-Rum Mochaccino

The ultimate combination for all chocolate lovers out there!

Ingredients:

- Single espresso

- ¼ cup heavy cream, whipped
- 1 tablespoon chocolate
- 1½ teaspoons brandy
- 1½ teaspoons crème de cacao
- 1½ teaspoons rum
- 3 ounces milk, steamed
- Ground cinnamon
- Ground nutmeg
- Thin wafer, for garnish

Directions:

1. Combine the espresso, brandy, rum, crème de cacao, and chocolate syrup in a glass.
2. Put in 11 ounces steamed milk and 11 ounces milk foam.
3. Put on top the whipped cream, drizzle with cinnamon and nutmeg, and decorate with a wafer.

Yield: 1 Servings

Cappuccino Calypso

Coffee and rum goes great together!

Ingredients:

- Single espresso
- 1½ teaspoons rum
- 2 tablespoons Tia Maria
- 3 ounces milk, steamed

Directions:

1. Combine all the ingredients excluding the milk in a glass.
2. Put in 1½ ounces steamed milk and 1½ ounces milk foam.

Yield: 1 Servings

Grasshopper Cappuccino

A cool minty drink!

Ingredients:

- <u>Single espresso</u>
- ¼ cup heavy cream, whipped
- 1½ teaspoons crème de cacao
- 1½ teaspoons crème de menthe
- 3 ounces milk, steamed
- Fresh mint sprig, for garnish
- Sweetened chocolate powder

Directions:

1. Combine the espresso, crème de menthe, and crème de cacao in a glass.
2. Put in 1½ ounces steamed milk and 1½ ounces milk foam.
3. Put on top the whipped cream and chocolate powder and decorate with a fresh mint sprig.

Yield: 1 Servings

Variation: To make a Grasshopper Mochaccino, mix 1 teaspoon chocolate syrup into the milk before steaming it or mix the syrup into the espresso before mixing. Rest of the process is the same as above.

Cold Drinks Made with Brewed Coffee

The drinks that follow are made with cold coffee. They are good in every season!

Iced Amaretto — Brandy Coffee

Almond and brandy go great together!

Ingredients:

- ¼ cup heavy cream, whipped
- ¾ cup coffee Ice cubes
- 1 ounce amaretto
- 1 tablespoon brandy
- Sliced almonds, for garnish

Directions:

1. Put in the amaretto and brandy to the coffee.
2. Pour over ice, put on top the whipped cream, and decorate with sliced almonds.

Yield: 1 Servings

Blended Chocolate-Brandy Coffee

Brandy and chocolate taste awesome on a warm summer afternoon.

Ingredients:

- ½ cup coffee
- ½ cup milk
- 2 tablespoons brandy
- 2 tablespoons chocolate syrup
- Ice cubes

Directions:

1. Combine all the ingredients together in a blender for 15 to 20 seconds, or until foamy.
2. Pour over ice in a tall glass.

Yield: 1 Servings

Coffee-Rum Blended

A drink with smooth texture enhanced with rum!

Ingredients:

- ¼ cup coffee
- ¼ cup milk
- 1 scoop coffee ice cream
- 1½ tablespoons crème de cacao
- 1½ tablespoons rum

Directions:

1. Combine all the ingredients together in a blender.
2. Pulse for 15 to 20 seconds, or until smooth.

Yield: 1 Servings

Coffee Alexander

A coffee drink that packs a punch!

Ingredients:

- ½ cup heavy cream, whipped
- ¾ cup coffee
- 1 ½ tablespoons amaretto
- 1 ½ tablespoons Kahlúa
- 2 scoops chocolate ice cream
- Ice cubes
- Sweetened chocolate powder

Directions:

1. Combine the coffee, Kahlúa, amaretto, and ice cream in a blender.
2. Pulse for 15 to 20 seconds, or until smooth.
3. Pour over ice and put on top the whipped cream and chocolate powder.

Yield: 2 Servings

Variation: Substitute 2 scoops of vanilla ice cream for the chocolate. Rest of the process is the same as above, topping with a dash of ground nutmeg or cinnamon instead of sweetened chocolate powder.

Cold Drinks Made with Espresso

Unless otherwise specified, the following drinks are made with freshly made espresso and served instantly.

Kahlúa- Rum Chocolate Espresso Float

A cool and sweet treat, perfect for cooling down.

Ingredients:

- Double espresso, cold
- ¼ cup heavy cream, whipped
- 1 scoop chocolate ice cream
- 1 teaspoon Kahlúa
- 1 teaspoon rum
- Sweetened chocolate powder

Directions:

1. Combine the espresso, Kahlúa, and rum in a glass.
2. Put in the ice cream and put on top the whipped cream and chocolate powder.

Yield: 1 Servings

Kahlúa — Crème de Cacao Iced Cappuccino

A sweet, creamy, and cool coffee drink.

Ingredients:

- Single espresso
- ¼ cup heavy cream, whipped

- 1 ½ teaspoons crème de cacao
- 1½ teaspoons Kahlúa
- 3 ounces milk
- Ground cinnamon or sweetened chocolate powder
- Ice cubes

Directions:

1. Combine the espresso, milk, Kahlúa, and crème de cacao together and pour over ice.
2. Put on top the whipped cream and cinnamon or chocolate powder.

Yield: 1 Servings

Cocoa-Mint Espresso Shake

Cocoa, mint and vanilla taste great together!

Ingredients:

- Single espresso
- ¼ teaspoon crème de menthe
- 1 scoop vanilla ice cream
- 1 teaspoon crème de cacao

Directions:

1. Combine all the ingredients together in a blender.
2. Pulse for 15 to 20 seconds, or until smooth.

Yield: 1 Servings

Iced Brandy — Cointreau Espresso

This drink can be enjoyed hot and cold!

Ingredients:

- Double espresso, cold
- ¼ cup heavy cream, whipped
- 1 teaspoon brandy
- 1 teaspoon Cointreau
- Grated orange peel, for garnish
- Ice cubes

Directions:

1. Combine the espresso, brandy, and Cointreau and pour over ice.
2. Put on top the whipped cream and decorate with grated orange peel.

Yield: 1 Servings

Variation: For an Iced Brandy-Crème de Cacao Espresso, omit the Cointreau and substitute 1 teaspoon crème de cacao. Decorate with sweetened chocolate powder instead of grated orange peel.

Endnote

This is it! You've learnt all that I teach you. It is all up to you now. Use all that you've learnt int his book as a foundation of your own coffee-making journey. Experiment, try new things, keep recipes you like, and discard recipes you don't.

I would also greatly value your feedback on this book, so don't forget to leave a review on amazon!

Good Luck! Have Fun!

Printed in Great Britain
by Amazon